Contents

2-8
Introduction

9-24
Week 1
Zechariah & Elizabeth: Waiting in Hope

25-40
Week 2
Mary: Waiting in Weakness

41-54
Week 3
The Shepherds: Waiting in Company

55-67
Week 4
Simeon and Anna: Waiting in Worship

68-69
An Advent Prayer

70-85
Kid-size Devotions & Colouring Sheets

Introduction

My husband drove us home from the *Big Christmas Light Switch On*, with tingling toes and dripping noses, reeling from our first taste of the festivities–albeit in November.

"Mum, whyyyyyy do we have to wait for Advent to put up our Christmas tree?" a voice hollered from the black abyss of the back seat, obviously anticipating our next hit of magic.

It was the same question I answered every year, pretty much every day.

"Because Advent is how we prepare to celebrate Jesus at Christmas. Because, with all of the busy stuff going on, Advent signals that it's time to slow down and make room in our hearts for him. Because it's good to wait, honey."

I was tired of the 6394729 car questions, but the answer to this one was well-rehearsed.

Preparing, remembering, waiting–Advent was kind of my jam.

But that's when, if I'd been warm enough, a panicked bead of sweat would have dripped down the back of my neck. I looked at Paddy who was just trying to stay conscious at the wheel.

He responded with a nonchalant hug, a shell of a man after an altogether overstimulating evening.

I am a self-confessed Advent Nerd™. But on a dark drive along the M2, sneaking bites of chocolate with thawing hands, one child screaming and one asking for a bedtime story, Advent quietly snuck up on me.

The lights weren't up. The candles weren't lit. The number blocks weren't on display. The Advent devotional had yet to be purchased, or even chosen. It's typical, really. God's people had thousands of years to get ready and when the time had finally come, they still had no room at the inn.

As I made a last-minute decision to ditch the faff and read slowly through Luke 1-2 in December, this is the Jesus I met:

The One who stepped down so that I could give up. Give up striving, working, mustering my own strength, and playing catch up. The Lifter of my Head, the Person of Jesus—he is my first love. Not the lights, the candles, or any pretty devotional book (but it's okay if you think this book is particularly pretty).

Yes, Advent is about preparing, but we can't forget Jesus has already done it all. He has already prepared a place for us. A place at his table, a place in his arms. We just have to come.

I am yet to forget about Advent again. In fact, I find myself thinking about it all year round, constantly surprised at how the truths of Luke 1-2 continue to minister to my heart.

But let's be real: we want Christmas, not Advent. We want the celebration without the waiting. Christmas is a hard time to embrace the discipline of pausing and feeling our need. We have a million things to do. Gifts to buy, people to see, events to attend—Advent is almost incompatible with the pace of Christmas. It drives our kids crazy to open only one door or light one candle at a time. And it drives me crazy when an Amazon delivery takes two days instead of one.

But waiting is part of the job description as a Christian. We live in an everyday advent, longing for the second coming. It's tempting to believe that fleeing this broken world is the answer, but Advent not only reminds us of Jesus' first in-flesh arrival to that same broken world, but points ahead to his physical return when he will reign over this world forever. He will wipe away every tear and bring an end to our illness, grief, pain and heartache once and for all.

While this season is already filled with sweet sentiment, the discipline of Advent is crucial. As we wearily recover from a busy year of hard work, we need this blocked-off section of our calendars to remind us of the eclipsing truth: he is on his way.

Just in case you needed the reminder: the One who came will be faithful to come again. Let's allow ourselves to sit in the tension of the season, because Advent is a remembrance, but it is also a rehearsal.

In Luke 1:78-79, the people of Israel are portrayed as stranded and wandering in an empty, howling expanse of wilderness. The darkness is thick to touch. Rocks of fear trip their feet and the weight of hopelessness slows them down. A black sky presses down on them. They cannot bear to take one more step. But then, a glint of colour on the horizon.

The rising sun–the dawn of hope.

The Nitty Gritty Details

I didn't want this book to be something you have to check off a list every day of December. I didn't want you to have a rushed quippy thought to read between the chaos–or read a whole bunch in catch-up mode like I usually do.

I wrote it to be a companion, a cosy hug. This book is the product of an Advent year in my life, one particularly filled with waiting and *seemingly* unanswered prayer. (I also wrote the bulk of this during the wait of a first trimester in pregnancy, so certain sentences will forever and always give me a wave of nausea.)

For you, I hope this devotional can be a forced break and a breather. There are four chapters–one for each week of Advent and the content of each week is broken down into three parts. But you can dip in and out in whatever way works best for you.

As my words slowly walk you through this Advent season, I hope they will illuminate what is already in God's word.

Whether you are a *savour every word at snail's pace* kind-of-person, or a *binge it all at once* kind-of-person (I am a bit of both), the freedom is yours.

My only recommendation is that you begin by spending some time in Luke 1-2 on its own. Spend a day or two highlighting, wandering, exploring and falling down rabbit holes. Don't be tempted to rush ahead—God can handle our questions. Get his words under your skin.

Each week begins with a personal story as I press you to see the ways in which these eternal truths relate to your real life —partly because I'm a storyteller at heart, but also because that is how I make sense of God's story in my own life. I will attempt to guide you through *the waiting stories* of Zechariah and Elizabeth, Mary, the Shepherds, and Simeon and Anna–followed by some reflection questions at the end of each week. Finally, just for fun, I've added four short kids devotions with corresponding colouring sheets, illustrated by my talented friend, Lucy.

Full disclosure: writing for children is definitely not in my comfort zone, but I love re-telling God's story in a way that speaks to others--no matter their age. I love watching the recognition on their faces when they 'get it'. Hopefully, if you have small people in your life, I have done the hard work for you on this one.

In our home we want to keep things simple and sweet in this season, so we plan to do one of the kid-size devotions each Sunday evening of Advent—maybe with a candle and some hot chocolate. But please use them how you see fit, or ignore them altogether!

Finally, I've collated a gorgeous Spotify playlist which you can find under the name *Awaiting the Rising Sun*. Yes, it is several hours long. No, Silent Night and Away in Manger are not on it. (Because I *need* to know the birth of Christ was not silent. More on that later.)

Thank you for choosing to hold my little book in your hands. It means more to me than you will ever know. I'm fully aware there are approximately one billion Advent resources out there and I am genuinely doing a happy dance that you've chosen to walk through this one with me. I wish we could talk about Jesus over coffee or hot chocolate every single time you read it, but instead, I would be delighted to read a message or email if you fancy sharing.

So, here's to Jesus, the rising sun–who emptied himself, so we could be full.

Full of everlasting life, peace in trials, freedom from sin's grip and guilt, and hope for our heavy hearts.

"Because of the tender mercy of our God, by which the rising sun will come to us from heaven to shine on those living in darkness and in the shadow of death, to guide our feet into the path of peace"

Luke 1: 78-79

Week 1

Scripture: Luke 1:5-25 & 57-80

Zechariah & Elizabeth: Waiting in Hope

Introduction

I'm grabbing a few forgotten grocery items at the shop when I get the call. With a punnet of half-price grapes in my hand and an ever-growing grocery list in my head, I almost don't pick up. I mean, I don't usually pick up when she calls. I usually let it go to voicemail. And then I panic and prepare myself for about half an hour before calling her back. I don't like being caught off guard–especially with a part-baby-part-orangutan hanging out of the shopping trolley and an eight-year-old with bionic hearing just a few feet ahead.

But on this occasion, something makes me answer the phone. Maybe I've become a fully grown adult with control over how conversations affect me. Or maybe, I just want it to be over with. Maybe, the dread rising in my heart is already too much to bear.

For the last twenty months, my husband, Paddy has been going through the process of adopting my son. When I say Paddy has been going through the process, I really mean our whole family have been through some hardcore emotional upheaval. What began as a short and simple celebration to affirm a relationship that already exists, has become a complicated hike through a dark valley of social workers and solicitors and unexpected news and guardians and court hearings.

The endless waiting has brought me to my knees in permanent surrender.

"Hello?" I answer, trying to sound cheery and not at all anxious.

It's the guardian, who represents my son's voice in court. She's extremely likeable, but it still bothers me that this likeable stranger gets to be his voice.

She makes casual conversation as if we've been friends our whole lives. At this point, we kind of have. Clocking eyes with my eldest who has now realised I'm on the phone, I try to usher the conversation towards the main thing.

"Rebecca, I wanted to tell you we now have a date for the final adoption hearing. It's nearly over. I wanted to be the first to tell you that. The end is in sight."

There's a long pause. Too long.

"Oh... thanks. That's great," is all I manage to say, because I've learned the hard way not to cling to dates, like a life raft, always slightly out of reach.

"I thought you'd be more excited," she gives a hearty laugh and I can hear the sympathetic smile in her voice, filling me with guilt.

I sigh.

"I'm just... I'm afraid to get my hopes up."

Part 1
vs.1-4

When we enter into the story of Zechariah and Elizabeth, God has been silent for four hundred years. A thick, suffocating silence. Or so it seems.

The Roman Empire is running the show and the Jewish community is learning how to live under foreign occupation and oppression. There have been zero prophets, zero words from God, and zero fresh hope to cling to. Not since the prophet Malachi, who finished the Old Testament by promising God's people, *"...the sun of righteousness shall rise with healing in its wings. You shall go out leaping like calves from the stall"* (Malachi 4:2).

At this point, there is no healing or leaping in sight. Only waiting.

Cue: me *leaping* to get to Zechariah and Elizabeth.

Skip the waiting and get straight to the good bit? *Sounds good to me.*

But there's something Luke wants us to know first: King Herod is on the throne (v.5). And if you've met Herod in a children's Christmas nativity, he doesn't come across as all that threatening. Slightly unhinged and power-hungry maybe, but he certainly doesn't get more than a second thought from most of us.

Herod the Great's tyrannical reign is marked by bloodshed, cruelty, and vengeance. He goes down in secular history as 'great' in that he builds a lot of stuff, but his vindictive leadership is laced with paranoia. As long as he lives, no woman's honour is safe and no man's life is secure. He has no problem killing off his wife and other family members in order to bring about his purposes, and the word on the street is that it's safer to be Herod's pig than to be Herod's son.

Later in Luke, he demands all boys under the age of two are murdered, simply because he cannot gain access to young Jesus. But in Jewish historical records, this atrocity is so minor in the vast scheme of bloodshed during his time, that it isn't even recorded. It isn't front-page news, just a minor story on page 27. His reign is one of Hitler-eqsue proportions.

So, on top of God's silence, there is this deep societal darkness. These might be the most corrupt, hopeless, desperate days that men and women can remember. The Israelites cry out, *where is God now? Has he abandoned us? Has he forgotten his promises? When will he save us?*

God, are you even there?

None of the events during Herod's reign take God by surprise. It is in the midst of this longing and waiting that dawn is about to break. God is about to speak. Heaven is getting ready to touch Earth. Eternity is about to invade time. God is about to make good on the promise he made all the way back in Eden.

The camera sweeps from the palace of this tyrannical oppressor, Herod to the lowly home of a humble priest, Zechariah. Heralding from the countryside, with a modest background, and zero pomp or prestige, Zechariah is the most unassuming and unimpressive of men. In all of the political ebb and flow, God is bringing down rulers from their thrones and lifting up the humble (v.52). He is at work in ways that are not immediately apparent.

You see, we can't skip straight to the good bit. The only way is *through*. Because God has been at work this whole time– in the deep societal darkness, in the debilitating heartache and devastation, in the spiritual desert; he has been moving in unexpected ways.

Believe me when I say *this world terrifies me*. I am not trying to slap a positive Sunday smile on all of our faces. I can't help but look around and fear for tomorrow, never mind fear for the future; to wonder why I brought children into all of this; to feel like God has left the building. Fed up waiting, I wrestle for control, only to find I am powerless and paralysed. I can't even pick up the phone.

I don't know why God doesn't intervene in the ways I think he should, but I do know this; he is always at work in ways I cannot see with earthly eyes. The fears of this world and my *own little world* keep me from lifting my eyes to see what God has planned and promised. But if this Advent story is anything to go by, he is at work even in the emptiest darkness. There is a glow of light along the horizon. There is a hue of hope as night draws to a close.

Part 2
vs.5-24

Zechariah and Elizabeth are that beautiful, godly older couple you hope will invite you over for dinner. You long for them to scoop you under their wing and shower you with all of their hard-earned wisdom.

Zechariah is a priest from the eighth division of Abijah, and Elizabeth is the daughter of a priest. Notice the words used to describe the couple–*righteous* or *upright* before God and *blameless* (v.6). Not perfect or sinless, but *faithful*. They are constant and steadfast in serving the Lord.

And this is what makes their childless state all the more shocking and confusing to those around them. Infertility in any culture is heartache, but in ancient Hebrew culture, it is considered a punishment. A *disgrace* as Elizabeth herself later puts it.

In verse 7, Luke tells us Elizabeth is barren and they are both advanced in years, to make sure we know *all hope* is gone. Other translations say they are *stricken* in years (KJV). Everyone around them is having grandchildren, maybe great-grandchildren, and it's suffice to say, a baby is not on their retirement radar.

So, not only is there a cultural darkness around them, but there is a personal dark shadow over their home. Their lives are marked by this private suffering, this unfulfilled longing. Their wrinkled, worn faces will never look new life in the eyes and see their own reflected back. With empty arms they carry on, serving and waiting, for the relief that comes first: salvation or heaven.

***

In Zechariah's line of work there are many priests, but there are not enough sacred duties for everyone. So, while Zechariah serves in the temple twice a year, as one of eighteen thousand priests, only once in his life will he get to offer incense in the Holy Place. In fact, some priests will never receive the privilege.

This moment is already the high point in Zechariah's career. This is the greatest honour of his whole earthly existence, and since we are familiar with the Christmas story, we know *God's Grace* is about to blow it out of the water. Zechariah is probably already overwhelmed and excited, and somewhere in the back of his mind, he is probably already thinking *I can't wait to tell Elizabeth.*

But oh, *he has no idea.*

When Zechariah steps into the Holy Place, his eyes must catch the crimson, blue, royal purple and gold cherubim embroidered in the Holy of Holies. Directly in front of him is the horned golden altar of incense. To his left there is the table of shewbread, and to his right stands the golden candlestick (Exodus 30:1-10; 37:25-29).

Like Simeon in chapter two, it is likely that Zechariah prays for the promised saviour. His longing prayer curls towards heaven along with the incense when it happens: a terrifying angel of the Lord appears before him. And the angel was none other than Gabriel, who appeared to Daniel in Babylon over 500 years beforehand. *Of course.*

And after hundreds of years of silence, God speaks.

First, Gabriel tells Zechariah not to be afraid. (Angels in the bible always say *don't be afraid*–Oh! no problem, Gabe!)

He continues: Zechariah's prayer has been answered and he and Elizabeth are going to have a son who will prepare the way for the Messiah, like the prophet Elijah. He will bring joy and gladness to his elderly parents. He will be great, but the One for whom he prepares the way will be even greater. This will fulfil the promise made by God hundreds of years before through the prophet Malachi.

"Behold, I will send you Elijah the prophet before the great and awesome day of the LORD comes. And he will turn the hearts of the fathers to their children and the hearts of children to their fathers..." (Malachi 4:5-6a).

How can I know this is true? Zechariah questions, asking for a sign.

Zechariah always gets a bad rap in this passage. We gawk in horror at his *doubt* or his *unbelief*. The supernatural awesome messenger from heaven standing right in front of him is a pretty solid sign, right?

But what I see, is a weary man who is afraid to get his hopes up.

Maybe, Zechariah finds this news so hard to believe as he stopped praying for a son many years ago. Maybe, he can't remember the last time he prayed for a son. Maybe, his hopes have been raised and flattened too many times before. Maybe, the routine of all his priestly activity has caused him to forget that God keeps his promises. Maybe, just a few minutes ago he was praying for the salvation of God's people, for the long-awaited Messiah, and maybe he doesn't dare believe he and his aging wife will have a part to play. Maybe, he can't get his head around this *grace*.

That's why his son's name will be *John*, meaning *God has been gracious*.

Zechariah certainly receives a sign. He is made mute– the penalty for his disbelief. But during the next nine months of silence, he will have plenty of time to exercise his spiritual muscle of faith.

Meanwhile, outside the temple, everyone is becoming restless. Zechariah had one job to do and it shouldn't have taken this long. *What's the hold-up?* When he finally appears, making signs and gestures and zero sound, they have no way of knowing what has actually happened, but they know it is *something significant*.

Trying to fill Elizabeth in on the news must be excruciating. But sure enough, in fulfilment of God's promise, Elizabeth conceives. We don't know why she keeps herself hidden for five months, and we can only speculate, but perhaps she waits until her pregnancy is visible. Perhaps she is simply bedridden with nausea, or perhaps the next time she steps out in public, she wants to be sure she can do so without shame.

Her unfruitful womb experiences maternal bloom, her decaying body produces flourishing life. Misery turns to hope, mourning turns to dancing–a glimpse of the resurrection to come.

Part 3
vs.57-80

After nine months of waiting, which probably feels longer to Elizabeth than the last four hundred years, she finally gives birth to a baby boy.

And just like any other birth since the beginning of time, the whole world stops to hold its breath, even just for a moment. The labouring, the hoping, the wondering, the fearing; all finds its focus in the scrunched up face of this tiny little person squawking for milk. God's love is written in the folds of rosy skin and fluttering of sticky eyes, and somehow, every hope and dream turns to reality. Before that reality becomes a daily weight to carry, every child is a bundle of possibilities, a fresh canvas waiting to be a masterpiece.

And just like any other newborn in the history of humanity, folks seem to have an opinion about the name. Anyone who has ever had the privilege of naming a child knows the golden rule: *don't say the name too soon*. It's safest to stay quiet, at the risk of Great Aunt Sally putting you off the name you've grown to cherish.

But being a real moment in time with real men and real women, Zechariah and Elizabeth receive a real reaction from their busybody family and friends when they announce the name of John. Not accepting Elizabeth's answer as acceptable, they turn to her husband, who shuts down the conversation.

"His name is John." Fullstop. End of discussion.

It seems in the last nine months, Zechariah has been contemplating everything. Imagine the emotion of the moment as he scribbles on the tablet. Imagine what has been happening in his heart.

God has been revealing himself. Once again, he is working in the so-called silence. And upon his belief, Zechariah's penalty is *immediately* lifted. Grace immediately ensues. And praise is immediately lifted.

On this occasion, we might expect Zechariah to erupt in song about the wonderfulness of his precious new son, but instead Zechariah, filled with the Holy Spirit, erupts in a song filled with praise to God from beginning to end.

Praise to God for keeping his promise to David, praise to God for keeping his promise to Abraham, praise to God for keeping his promise to Zechariah in giving him his son John, the forerunner; and finally, praise to God for the coming of *the rising sun* (v.78 NIV).

He looks back on how the tender mercy of God delivered his people from the oppression of Egypt, and looks forward to the tender mercy of God doing this again, through Jesus. But this time, they will be delivered from the spiritual oppression of sin once and for all (v.74).

John's task as the mouthpiece of God is to bring to his people *knowledge of salvation* (v.77). In their worldly and political aspirations, the Jews have lost their knowledge of salvation and have substituted vain dreams and all kinds of empty hopes in place of it. This is not *head knowledge* or *book knowledge*, kept at arm's length like a religious education lesson at school. No, this is an experiential grasp of what God has done in Christ. This knowledge of salvation causes a revolution in the heart and mind so that one will ever be the same again.

Zechariah ends his song with praise for the imminent sunrise: *"because of the tender mercy of our God, by which the rising sun will come to us from heaven to shine on those living in darkness and in the shadow of death, to guide our feet into the path of peace"* (vs.78-79).

Luke portrays the people of Israel as stranded and wandering in an empty, howling expanse of wilderness. The darkness is thick to touch. Rocks of fear trip their feet and the weight of hopelessness slows them down. A black sky presses down on them. They cannot bear to take one more step. *But then*, a glint of colour on the horizon.

The rising run–the dawn of hope.

Here is the fulfilment of the final Old Testament prophecy we noted at the beginning: *"...the sun of righteousness shall rise with healing in its wings. You shall go out leaping like calves from the stall."* (Malachi 4:2).

In all the advances of the 20th Century, humanity still exists in a deep weariness of life, wandering in an empty wilderness and in the shadow of death. If we don't know the ache of an empty womb, we know the ache of an empty bed, an empty room, an empty mind, or the quiet of an ordinary empty Tuesday.

But this is not the end of the story.

As we walk through Advent, and through many ordinary Tuesdays the rest of the year, we are bold enough to hope.

Not because we cling to our own human resourcefulness. We do not cling to temporary christmassy hype. Like pieces of thin ice shattering beneath our feet, we do not cling to end-dates, phone calls, answers or positive platitudes; we cling to the promises of God. The One who broke into the darkness of eternity, has authority over every inch of darkness in our lives.

The One who kept his promise to come will keep his promise to come again.

And one day soon we will step out of time into eternity to see the Son in all his glory. Then we will fully understand how the tender mercy of God has authored our every step.

The sun has risen.

We wait in hope.

Questions for Reflection & Prayer

1. We are not promised certainty in our circumstances, but we are promised certainty in the God of our circumstances. You can be honest with God: are there situations in which you feel hopeless or you doubt God's presence in the darkness? How does this passage encourage you that God is not silent in your circumstances?

2. Read the following promises. Write out a prayer, handing your circumstances over to God, confessing your doubt and asking him to help you put your hope in him. James 1:5, 1 Corinthians 10:13, John 10:28-29, Hebrews 13:5, Philippians 1:6, and Luke 12:40.

Someday, we will fully understand how the tender mercy of God has authored our every step.

Week 2

Scripture: Luke 1:26-56

Mary: Waiting in Weakness

Introduction

I'm twenty-two years old when I feel weakness for the very first time.

It's a black morning in early November and condensation slides down the broken bedroom window that permanently sits ajar. I don't have money to buy heating oil and I'm further from student loan day than I want to think about. I don't want to think. Period.

I try to get out of bed but every inch of my body recoils at the thought of the day ahead. At the thought of living. My three year old son snores lightly beside me and I want to disappear into the duvet beside him. To disappear. Full stop.

But I need to get this precious boy to nursery, not that he's had enough sleep, anyway. I don't know it yet, but the image of us sitting on his bedroom floor the night before, limbs entangled, both of us weeping after another violent tantrum; will be ingrained in my mind forever. Like a broken etch-a-sketch that never erases.

I want to cancel today. To cancel life. But I'm in the final year of my degree, and every day is a day closer to a deadline. Emphasis on *dead*.

Help me sit up, Lord. Please.

I hold my breath and sit up.

Help me get out of this bed.

I hold my breath a little longer. I wait. I pray again.

Help me, please. I need you. I can't do this.

Up until this point I've taken pride in my ability to endure. Teenage pregnancy? Raising a child alone? Studying and working? *No problem.* But if I admit I might not have it in me to do this myself, then I prove *them* right. I don't know who *they* are, but I've been following Jesus for a couple of years at this point and their opinion is still louder than his most of the time.

When my feet finally hit the floor of my bedroom, I think of the ten-minute coffee I had with a friend in between classes recently. She is the first person to mention the D word. Depression. My doctor agrees. It's a work in progress. It's likely it always has been and always will be.

At the end of the day, I leave the library earlier than usual, resolving to do more work after my son's bedtime. We head for the forest, craving the therapeutic crunch of leaves beneath our feet. Instead, we're shuffling through post-autumn sludge when we see a crowd of people gathered to watch trees being chopped in the distance. My son points to the tallest, thickest, sky-scraping tree and asks why it hasn't been chosen.

"The loggers know it's rotting on the inside," the man beside us answers, "the wind will probably blow it over anyway."

"Wow," my son says with incredulous eyes.

I smile, relating to the fragile bark that could crumble at any minute. The strong, capable appearance masking its internal weakness. We walk on, taking another route.

I'm not hollow though, I say to no one. *The Apostle Paul would say I'm more like a jar of clay* (2 Cor. 4:7).

I am a dry, potentially-cracked jar of clay; but I hold the treasure of the gospel inside. I am an unlikely, weak vessel, unfit to hold such glorious treasure, and yet this is how God shows that the surpassing power belongs to him and not to me.

When I have nothing left of myself to give, God's strength upholds me and is displayed for all the world to see.

And sometimes it is a very powerful thing to get out of bed.

Part 1
v26-38

Greetings, O favoured one. The Lord is with you! Gabriel announces, in all of his usual splendour and terror.

Here's how you might expect May to respond: *Well, it's about time you showed up–I've been waiting for someone to see my potential after all I've done for the Lord. Don't you agree I'm a great candidate for his purposes?*

But that's not how the story goes. The Mary we know is disquieted at heart. She wonders why on earth he calls her, of all people, favoured. She ponders on the reason for this encounter and why he is about to give *her*, of all people, a special task. She knows she is an unlikely candidate for a special visit from Gabriel; an unlikely recipient of God's special favour and special presence; an unlikely vessel for God's abundant power.

We immediately think of Gabriel's visit with Zechariah: the old, wise priest serving in the temple in Jerusalem. But this time Gabriel skips the temple, the holiest place in Israel.

He skips Judea, the heartland of God's work through the centuries. And he heads for Nazareth, a non-place, totally disregarded by the Jews because of its mongrelised population.

Can anything good come from Nazareth? Nathaniel blurts out in the Gospel of John.

This town is nothing more than a shoddy halfway stop between two port cities, overrun by gentiles and roman soldiers.[1] Gabriel skips the homes of the scholarly, the affluent, and the wealthy, and he heads for the lowly home of an unaccomplished, probably illiterate probably- fourteen year old girl who, in the eyes of the world is a nobody from

---

[1] R Kent Hughes, *Luke*, p. 29

a nothing town in the middle of nowhere.

Don't miss the unexpectedness of God choosing one so unlikely and so unimportant. Mary is poor, weak and insignificant. We are so familiar with the narrative we almost think *of course he goes to the wee virgin Mary in her blue dress.*

But this is shocking. This is impossible. *The greatest news ever proclaimed on earth comes to the humblest of people.* This is how God moves in the world–in those who recognise their weakness and need for him.

We are not a culmination of our age, weight, height, hobbies, career, and family background; how we respond to God is a true portrait of who we are. And Mary responds in beautiful humility.

She is told she will conceive a son and call his name Jesus (meaning the Lord is salvation). And there are three qualifications for this new son of hers: he will be great, he will be the Son of God, and he will have the throne of David and reign forever.

If the shock hasn't completely taken over her mind, Mary knows Gabriel is winking at God's promise in 2 Samuel:12-13, a promise that reverberates throughout the Old Testament and the scripture readings Mary hears at home and at the temple.

"When your days are over and you rest with your ancestors, I will raise up your offspring to succeed you, your own flesh and blood, and I will establish his kingdom. He is the One who will build a house for my Name, and I will establish the throne of his kingdom forever."

Mary, young little virgin girl, you are the one who will bear the One you have been waiting for.

And naturally, Mary wonders about the logistics. She is a virgin. *How* will this happen?

Are you catching the similarities between this scene and the one we looked at in the last chapter? In both, Gabriel is sent by God. In both, he brings a birth announcement. In both, the birth conception is miraculous. And in both, the recipient is puzzled.

But here, there is a difference. While Mary doesn't quite anticipate a virgin conception (*who would?*), Zechariah asked for a sign. He needed proof. He needed something tangible to hold on to. The difference is belief. Old, wise Zechariah has all the credentials of faith, but it is teenage Mary who believes.

The answer to *how?* is God's power. The power of the Most High will overshadow her (v.35). The word overshadow is used in the Old Testament when God's presence is in the temple, and the glory of God that fills the temple is the same glory of God that fills Mary. There is no greater power that could dwell in a weaker vessel.

And the answer to *how?* is Grace. God's Grace is not a cute, weak, happy little thing.

It is power. It is the power of the Gospel that brings salvation (Romans 1:16). It is the same power we receive when we experience the birth of Christ within us in the 21st Century. It is the same miraculous work of the Holy Spirit that gives us new life from above–something we cannot do for ourselves–something palpable and living and growing–something we can believe in. *For nothing is impossible with God* (v.37).

The exchange ends with Mary calling herself a servant of the Lord, which literally translates to slave–total belonging to Jesus. It would be extremely understandable if she said

[2] R Kent Hughes, *Luke*, p. 35

thanks but no thanks. But instead, she surrenders herself to him. The mother of Christ is already a disciple of Christ. And in her poverty of spirit, in her lack of any worldly power or strength, in her utter neediness and weakness; her humble heart is not only open to God's Grace but longs for it.

Let it be known–Mary will not have an easy life from this point on. She is betrothed to be married but the betrothal process in her culture is so binding it takes a divorce to end it. She is bound to Joseph in every way except flesh.

Mary is not a young woman in her mid-twenties planning a wedding and posting photographs of her engagement ring on Instagram. This is a highly sacred time. Her news will bring torrential shame upon her and her family and people will assume her son is an illegitimate child. She will be questioned and misunderstood; she will suffer and endure; she will come to the end of her own strength.

But there, she will throw herself into the arms of the One she now carries. Not because she is superficial or self-sufficient, but fully surrendered.

Part 2
v39-45

Mary didn't ask for a sign, but God still gave her one: *Elizabeth*. And while Mary's pregnancy is a different kind of miracle from the one received by her relative, it bears parallel testimony to God's power. Mary probably clings to this encouragement as she makes hasty arrangements with her parents, and travels the eighty-ish miles to the countryside of Judea. She just can't wait to get there. Like any woman, her mind is spinning. She needs to go and talk to someone about this situation.

And after a three or four-day journey, she arrives; her young, unannounced silhouette appearing in the old couple's doorway.

This is more than a prenatal catch-up. Every woman throughout Jewish history has been wondering *will my child be the one who undoes this curse?*

This is more than *boy or a girl? How many kicks? Any cravings?* Although I believe with all of my heart that these things are very much a part of it. But no, this is the meeting of two women caught up in God's divine plot to save the lost.

This is a victory cry; this is a trumpet call of welcome for the power and wonder carried in the wombs of these women. This is grandmotherly Elizabeth, great with child, age lines erased by pregnancy's spring, standing beside the virgin mother, ministering to her.

Before Elizabeth even has a chance to respond to Mary's *hello*, her baby responds for her. In her womb, *John* leaps. Remember when Malachi said there would be leaping like calves from the stall when the sun rises? Any expectant mother can relate to the prenatal vault Elizabeth must feel. But unlike the backflips I have felt with all of my babies,

Elizabeth's movement comes from a prophet. John the Baptist's ministry is beginning three months before he is even born.

At this stage, John is about nine inches long and weighs about one and a half pounds. His skin is translucent. He has fingernails and toe prints and sometimes he opens his eyes for brief periods. And yet, in the watery darkness of the womb, *he experiences the emotion of delight at meeting the light of the world.*

Without having seen or heard anything about Mary at all, Elizabeth finds herself perceiving perfect clarity. Filled with the Holy Spirit, she translates her baby's tumbling and she shouts for joy, affirming Mary's wonderful secret.

And probably loud enough for her muted unbelieving husband to hear in the next room, she assures Mary she is blessed because she *believed*.

Mary's greatest blessing doesn't come from being the mother of Jesus, but through her faith in him.

The visit with Elizabeth lasts about three months, so Mary may or may not be there for the birth of John the Baptist. I can very easily imagine her wanting to stay, but I can just as easily imagine her wanting to get home; in her stage of pregnancy, she may not feel up to dealing with all of Zechariah and Elizabeth's visits from family and friends.

Oh, how Mary must feel cared for. She could share Gabriel's words with her relative, but she could not be expected to fully understand or articulate the mystery. And even if she could, who would believe her? But Elizabeth does. During the biggest unexpected challenge of her young life so far, here is an older, godly woman to pray with, to discuss the scriptures with, to talk about birth and babies and bumps with.

God, in his mercy, gives her a friend to share her mutual belief, mutual experiences, and mutual hope. What a tender balm to Mary's soul. What *kindness*.

Part 3
v46-56

Mary's mind is full of the scripture she has heard at worship or at home throughout her life, so when the Holy Spirit comes upon her, she takes what she holds in her heart and weaves it into a beautiful tapestry of praise. Her lips declare her devotion. It is a song of overflowing thankfulness erupting from God's overflowing generosity. There are three themes interwoven through Mary's worship, and actually, throughout this whole Advent study: *God is mindful. God is mighty. God is merciful.*

Mary's song mirrors Hannah's song in 1 Samuel 2:1-10, but there is a difference in tone. While Hannah's is a shout of triumph, Mary's is a humble contemplation of the mercies of God. *Mary's humble state* (v.48) is not her personal childlessness, as had been Hannah's, but rather the nation of Israel's childlessness as it awaits the birth of a deliverer.

In her humble state, in her weakness, in her lack of power or riches or strength or reputation, she knows that neither she nor her people can do anything to bring about their own salvation.

Like Hannah, Mary throws herself upon the mercy of God as the only one who can help. Christ comes to those who realise their need, who know they cannot save themselves.

Those with no strength within themselves.

God has not forgotten the promise made to Abraham in Genesis 12 and 17. Generations rose and generations left, prophets came, and grandparents passed on, little ones rose to positions of influence; and still the people of God held on to this covenant promise that God made to their forefather, Abraham: *through your seed, all the nations of the earth will be blessed.* They told one another not to give up. They encouraged one another: *God is mindful, God is mighty, God is merciful.*

He saved them before, and here he is to save them again, once and for all. But not with political, economic, or military power like they expect. God's strength is not revealed in celebrity status that keeps him at arm's length. His mighty power does not come from wealth or platform. He does not make himself so important that we have to go through various channels to get to him. No, God's power is revealed in his intimacy with us. C. S. Lewis talks about a God who has landed on an enemy-occupied planet in human form.[3]

As a mighty warrior, he turns attitudes upside down. He takes what society, what culture, what men and women see as strength, and demolishes it. Money, sex, relationships, careers; this invasion of God in our lives shows where true riches lie. He scatters those who are proud, who think they don't need a saviour.

He brings down the rulers from their thrones and the empires of the world will eventually crumble to nothing. There is only one kingdom that will last forever and ever. And there is only one king, one majesty before whom we ought to bow.

Mary's song is the story of God's people, an account of God's absolute commitment, his persistent refusal to wash his hands of a wayward people; until eventually Jew and Gentile, male and female, slave and free, will stand together around the throne of God and declare *our God is mighty to save, and his mercy has been extended to us, his humble servants, from one generation to another* (v.50).

Mary, an unlikely vessel for God's power, will cling to these words. Her son will be great, but in the eyes of the world, she no longer will be. She will be shunned, shamed and

---

[3] C.S Lewis, *Mere Christianity*

disregarded.

Mary will become a mother to Mercy, and womb to the Way, the Truth and the Life. But she will birth her son in blood, pain and anguish, like every cursed daughter of Eve. She will see her face in his. And someday, she will stand below the cross and watch her son's face as he dies in blood, pain and anguish, defeating the very curse that enchains her.

This Advent, and all year round, and for the rest of our lives, we wait in weakness.

Because in our weakness, God's power and presence are on display. In our weakness, God exposes our pride, selfishness, greed, laziness and thanklessness. In our weakness, we look at the cross and know we are nothing but Christ is everything. In our weakness, we show the world we have hope beyond our present pain.

And in our weakness, God is mindful; God is merciful; and God is mighty.

Questions for Reflection & Prayer

1. Spend some extra time reading through and comparing Mary's song and Hannah's song in 1 Samuel 2:1-10. Circle or list all the attributes of God in both. What picture do these women paint of God? Based on your own relationship with God and how you have seen him work in your life, how would you describe him in song?

2. If you received a terrifying visit from Gabriel, would you question like Zechariah, or humbly surrender like Mary? Where in your life are you attempting to carry on in your own strength instead of throwing yourself into the arms of the One who can carry you through?

3. Mary was told that she was "blessed" above all women, but later she was told that a sword would pierce through her soul (Luke 2:34–35). In what way does knowing that Mary suffered for her faith, though she was blessed, encourage you today? If you have children or loved ones, you know what it is to hold them, to look into their eyes and want to protect them from pain. How does Mary's faith help you today?

4. In what situation do you need to be reminded that God is mindful, merciful, and mighty? Is there a friend you can encourage with this truth?

In our weakness,
God is mindful;
God is merciful;
and
God is mighty.

Week 3

Scripture: Luke 2:1-38

The Shepherds: Waiting in Company

Introduction

The vibrating alarm clock still reverberates through my body as I descend one stair at a time. I successfully avoid the creaks in the floorboards but I fear the creaks in my body will wake everyone up, anyway.

Wait, why doesn't the kitchen smell welcoming?

Ugh, I didn't set the timer on the coffee machine last night.

I add one heap of coffee for every hour my chesty child was up during the night with a cough. *Is that a wheeze rising in my own chest?*

I stretch to the top cupboard for the vitamins. My fingers instinctively scrape the sleepy crust from the corners of my eyes. I mentally run through this morning's to-do list while my brain waits for my body to catch up.

Make Reuben's packed lunch. Remember to fill in that form. Make breakfast. Reply to that email. Warm Weetabix for one and cold Weetabix for another. Today is Tuesday. Give Reuben an orange instead of an apple today. Should I put dinner in the slow cooker for later? Reply to that other email. Oh no, have I missed the deadline? Return that parcel. Ask Paddy if he filled in that other form. Is it my turn to do the tea and coffee at church this weekend? Don't be late to school again. Ask his teacher about that meeting. Book that gym class.

I rub the ache between my shoulder blades–a permanent pang of pain thanks to months of acrobatic breastfeeding positions. For the rest of today, I won't give the delicacy of my human body a second thought. But for now, I dream of climbing back into the womb of my duvet for just five more minutes.

My husband appears at the fridge door, rallying up a lunchbox and ironed shirt and coffee flask and rambling something incoherent about being late and traffic on the M2.

Suddenly the pace of my morning has picked up like a glass of cold water thrown in my face.

We kiss with all of our daily *goodbyes* and *I love you's*. I apologise for my morning breath. His stomach growls and we both laugh. With a sympathetic smile, I notice how puffy his eyes are. Our Tuesdays will see us take on extremely different roles, but our mornings unite us in our most basic selves. These are the moments that make us human. Human moments that are honest, human moments that are kind of gross, human moments weighed down by achy bodies.

Part 1
vs.1-5

It's time. And it almost seems like a coincidental quirk that Joseph and Mary end up *in the right place at the right time*. Caesar Augustus flexes his political muscle and so a village carpenter and his expectant teenage bride find themselves forced to travel to his hometown to be registered for taxation. Joseph's hometown being none other than Bethlehem, the City of David, where it was prophesied that the Messiah, David's greatest son, would be born. What a coincidence–oh wait.

The birth of Jesus, the greatest story of all time, is set against the backdrop of Caesar Augustus' reign. The adopted son of Julius Caesar, this so-called legend is heralded as the son of a *god* and worshipped as the instigator of the *Pax Romana*, a period of peace throughout the Roman Empire.

He has brought peace to the world, but Roman peace is an armed peace. An oppressive peace. Peace with a Roman foot planted squarely on the necks of their victims. Caesar's peace has been won on the battlefield at the cost of an enormous amount of bloodshed; producing terror, slavery, taxation and *silence*.

Herod's reign served as the chronological marker for John the Baptist's birth and now Caesar Augustus' reign serves as the chronological marker for John the Baptist's birth. The mention of these rulers is a painful reminder that Israel is still in captivity, even in their own land. They are *still waiting*.

Herod's heir will put John the Baptist to death and Caesar's heir, Pontius Pilate, will put Jesus to death. At the beginning and end of Luke's gospel, the Romans bookend the story doing the two things most hated by their subjects: taxation and crucifixion.

This is the world into which Jesus, the real Son of God, the real Saviour, and the bearer of real peace breaks into. As a vulnerable baby in the womb, of all things.

The angels proclaim *Christ the Lord* has come, not as a world ruler but a world redeemer, and he will knock all the other caesars and Augustuses off of their shelves. He comes with a peace that is far greater than the *Pax Romana*, a peace offered to all people, and the cost is borne by his bloodshed alone on the cross.

God uses the census decree of Caesar Augustus to fulfil what he had decreed centuries earlier; as unknown to them, all the kings and prime ministers and chancellors and chiefs of the world follow the sovereign decrees of our Father in heaven.

In his sovereignty over all nations and all events and all of history, God wields an empire to fulfill his word.

And if we are honest, it's hard to believe in this kind of sovereignty sometimes. Most of us aren't coming to this Advent study with Christmas cheer in our hearts. We are coming with personal pain on one hand and the public chaos of this world on the other. When we look down at our trembling hands, it's hard to believe every move is under the almighty hand of God.

As John Piper says (in a quote I have scribbled in an old journal and can't figure out where I heard or read it, but still cling to it with all my heart): *God is always doing 10,000 things in your life and you may be aware of about three of them.*

This is the God who writes our story: the One who is sovereign over history, the One who brings order to chaos, and the One who holds a plan for the powerless.

So, Joseph and Mary make the 80-mile, uncomfortable, full-term journey to Bethlehem. On the outside, they must look like helpless pawns caught in a movement of secular history, but Mary understands who she is and who God is. The baby nudging her ribs with his wriggly toes is not a Caesar, or a man trying to become a god, but the true God who has become man.

Part 2
vs.5-7

Maybe at first Mary isn't sure her pains are the pains. Maybe she hopes things will hold off until she's back home with her own mother. Maybe she keeps quiet until she can't anymore. Until every contraction rips through her body in a blanket of cold sweat. Until the doubt is shaken out of her with each wave of pain searing her cervix open. Until every exhausted pant is replaced with a cry of help to heaven.

Maybe she labours on the cold hard earth with the aroma of manure and straw filling her senses. Maybe after one final push, she reaches down to lift up her flailing newborn as his cry pierces the night. Maybe, in shock, she quickly checks the breathing of the ne who gave her breath.

Maybe. We don't know. We know only the facts–Luke's description of the birth is hauntingly simple. Normal, almost. *While they were there, the time came for the baby to be born, and she gave birth to her firstborn, a son, wrapped him in swaddling cloths and laid him in a manger because there was no place for them in the inn* (vs.6-7). An incredibly human moment.

The hands that hold the universe grab hold of Mary for comfort. The voice that spoke the world into existence can be heard crying in a feeding trough. The One who sustains every need now roots at Mary's breast for milk.

Into a huddle of animals, the promised Messiah enters creation among the creation. The limitless Lord of Lords and King of Kings is bound by the flesh of a helpless dependant. Fully God yet fully human, his little body is wrapped in swaddling cloths just as his adult body will be wrapped in linen cloth in the tomb.

We couldn't do it ourselves–we couldn't close the chasm between us and God. We couldn't bring ourselves back into a perfect Eden-esque relationship with him. Our limited minds couldn't fully understand what he spoke about Himself through his creation and his prophets. We couldn't make our own way to heaven and become like him and we couldn't enter his presence here on earth without fear of His glory obliterating us on the spot.

So in his mercy and kindness, he stepped down. He wanted us as his children, so he came to us and he became like us. On this side of the very first Christmas, we can see God's glory face to face in Christ and we can know His presence with us at all times.

For the weak, he became weak. For the grieving, he shed tears. For the low, he was brought low. For the broken, he allowed his body to be broken. For those who fail, he became part of a race of failures. For the hungry, he tasted hunger. For the shamed and the sinful, he became our sin and shame–*and he nailed it all to the cross*. Just as Jesus started his earthly life totally dependent on human breasts for milk, he ended his earthly life on the cross saying, "I am thirsty."

This time of year there is a lot of chat about *feeling christmassy*. Some years, it makes sense when we don't *feel it*. Life throws particularly hard situations our way. But other years, the Decembers keep coming and the feels just don't. Cosy decor? Check. Hallmark movies? Check. Festive family fun? Check. Matching pyjamas? Check check check– DARN IT WHY AREN'T THE MATCHING PYJAMAS WORKING?

No matter what we feel this December, we can turn to a tender-hearted Saviour who has felt it all. *We wait in good company.*

Cloaked in our flesh, Jesus felt the aches and pains of a tired body and experienced the backbreaking graft of working as a carpenter to provide for his family.

When his ministry began he didn't stay at the local Holiday Inn, but slept on the ground with rocks for pillows. He knew the suffocating darkness of grief and every day he came face to face with the physical and mental suffering of others.

He was not invulnerable to sin and temptation but he faced fully human temptations and overcame them. He was sufficiently different from us to save us. He was not under the power of the flesh, which warps human nature. He was led by the Spirit, which enabled him to checkmate satan.

Just as Mary laboured to bring God's son earthside, God the Son himself laboured on the cross to bring new life to earth. He tasted a cocktail of blood and vinegar as his naked body awaited its final breath, and he did so with joy so we could taste the freedom he fought so hard for.

This Advent comfort isn't just for a season. It isn't just a *hang in there–He's coming back again* kind of comfort. It is an ever-present comfort. It is a comfort that invades our waiting. That invades our pain. That invades every human moment of our lives. We do not wait alone.

Let's not be so distracted with feeling so *christmassy* that we forget to fall on our faces in *awe*.

Part 3
vs.8-21

By now we know that everything in Luke's story is backwards. The good news of the Messiah's arrival comes not to a princess, but to an obscure teenager; not to the home of the high and mighty, but to the home of a village carpenter; and now, not to the halls of academia, but to a field of unassuming shepherds. A field of shepherds who, as a class, are considered to be, well, scumbags. In fact, God dispatches his host of angels to a group who are despised by the religious orthodox or the *churchgoers*.

Because of their duties, this dishevelled group of ragamuffins miss far too many worship services and they tend to wash their hands a little less than the ceremonial and judicial laws would require of them.

The only people group lower than shepherds are lepers. The excluded shepherds are usually supposed to keep their flocks in the wilderness, so scholars believe that they were only this close to the town because they were pasturing flocks destined for temple sacrifices.

But God doesn't get the memo about the so-called social order, or at least he does and he's turning it on its head because the baby whom the angels come to announce will be the ultimate sacrificial lamb and will someday describe himself as none other than *the Good Shepherd who gives his life for his sheep.*

Before this group of men has a chance to consider what's happening, heaven's glory comes to earth, filling the night sky with light for a gallery of shepherds who are sitting in darkness.

The wonderful words of the angel, spoken not only for the shepherds but for all of us, announce the long-awaited *sun-*

rise from on high (1:78); the promised Saviour who can be found wrapped in swaddling clothes and lying in a manger.

The angels lift up their voices in cosmic-sized praise proclaiming *peace.* Not just peace for today, but a year-round peace. Not just a Christmas peace, but peace with God.

Yet the arrival of this baby will not bring peace on earth from wars or rumours of wars, earthquakes or floods, personal tranquillity or a life free from shock or tragedy. These pains will be the birth pangs of Jesus' second arrival.

For now, we see him come as the suffering servant (Isaiah 53). And in his second coming we'll see him come on the clouds as a victorious king. Then and only then will there be true peace on earth and the lion will lie down with the lamb (Isaiah 11:6).

***

When the angels have gone, no one asks what they should do next. There is no question about it. To Bethlehem they go, to see *this thing that has happened* (v.15). They don't go in order to believe, but *because* they believe.

And since Mary and Joseph are far from home and won't have many visitors from the neighbourhood, God arranges an alternative visit from these dusty-footed shepherds with their gnarled faces and sunburned leather skin.

When they catch a glimpse of the swaddled baby in the manger, they spread the incredible news: they were going about the routine of their lives and *God came*. Angels didn't bring good news to them because they were particularly pious, or uniquely religious. They came to their place of business while they were on the night shift.

Soon, their declaration moves to devotion as they head back to their responsibilities praising God. But their worship isn't a one-off hymnal around the fire pit, but a posture of worship that leaks into all of their lives. They will never be the same again.

The hard graft of shepherding will not change, and the daily grind and mundanity will not change, but God became human, and that changes everything.

Into the humiliation of their humanity, he came. He is with them in it all. The One who is worthy of worship, glory, and fanfare will spend decades in obscurity and ordinariness. The God-man will spend his days quietly, going to work, getting sleepy, and living a pedestrian life among average people. He'll spend his public ministry with the outcasts, the misfits and the losers. He will empathise with the most undignified human parts of their days.

Christ's ordinary years are part of our redemption story. Because of His humanity and those long, unrecorded years of Jesus' life, our small and ordinary lives matter. If Christ was a carpenter, all of us who are in Christ find that our work is sanctified and made holy. If Christ spent time in obscurity, then there is infinite worth found in obscurity. There is no task too small or too routine.

Christmas matters at 7 a.m. on an ordinary Tuesday morning. Christ's birth matters in every human moment. Some day the Shepherds will know the full significance of what they have seen in Bethlehem. But until then, they know this: God came to be with them, to be like them and until he comes again, *they wait in good company.*

Questions for Reflection & Prayer

1. When Mary gets to Bethlehem and there's no room, she must be tempted to doubt if God is really in control. Yes, he organised a census to get her there, but did he forget to organise a bed? The life of faith is full of these back and forward moments, attempting to trust God's purposes in the midst of confusing trials. In hindsight, where have you seen God work through experiences that seemed out of his control?

2. It turns out the shepherds weren't as cute as our primary school children wearing dressing gowns in the nativity with tea towels on their heads. The first worshippers at the manger look different to a typical crowd at Sunday morning worship in the 21st Century. Pray that God will give you the eyes to see people as he sees them. Trust me, it will kill prejudices you didn't even know you had.

3. How often do you think of Jesus' humanity–that he has felt everything we feel? That he came to be like us and with us? How does this truth transform the most ordinary or meaningless parts of your day?

For the weak, He became weak. For the grieving, He shed tears. For the low, He was brought low. For the broken, He allowed His body to be broken. For those who fail, He became part of a race of failures. For the hungry, He tasted hunger. For the shamed and the sinful, He became our sin and shame — and He nailed it all to the cross.

Week 4

Scripture: Luke 2:21:40

Simeon & Anna: Waiting in Worship

Introduction

I scrape the cold dirt from beneath my fingernails and curse my husband for putting the gardening gloves somewhere out of sight–or for losing them altogether. I wipe my sweaty hands on my jeans and open a text from the friend I hugged only yesterday.

Both of us sat cross-legged on my living room floor for hours, words and tears falling in a frenzy of grief.

"When will I feel joy again?" she asked over and over and over. But she didn't really want an answer. So together, we held her lament, while my toddler catapulted his body and a ball between us.

This morning, I found the mixture of seeds and bulbs at the bottom of a basket of toxic cleaning products under our kitchen sink. I wasn't surprised they'd been forgotten. The pic-n-mix of potential new life just screamed *good intentions.* Refusing to be mocked by my own failed to-do list, I marched my children straight outside and handed the big one a shovel.

As we excavate the garden for an appropriate planting bed, the prevalent questions are *when?* and *why?*

When will this be finished? When will they grow? Why do we have to look after them? Why do we have to wait so long?

Because this is what we do, my son.

Because golden daffodils only rise like the sun after months of a black Winter's wait. Because newborn babies only unfurl into the world after 40 weeks of a wet wait in the womb. Because my friend has to wait for the end of her grief, or at least a pause in her Winter, for the hint of some Spring joy to arrive. Because God's people still await the return of their King to reign over eternity.

Because this is what we do.

We dig our fingers in the dirt and we lay it all down and we wait for God to resurrect something good.

Part 1
vs.21-24

Newborn babies follow a loose (emphasis on loose) rhythm: eat, sleep, poo, cry, repeat. Things are less predictable for the recovering mother, with her body rearranged and her world recalibrated.

However, in the midst of Mary's raw newborn haze, she partakes in a different kind of rhythm: a religious one. The rituals of circumcision, naming, purification and presentation are a normal flow of events following the birth of a firstborn son in a Jewish family.

The book of Leviticus was a manual for Worship in Israel and according to its guidance, a woman was considered ceremonially unclean for one week after giving birth, followed by another thirty-three days of isolation. Double that if she gave birth to a girl. After the isolation period had passed, parents were instructed to go to the temple and sacrifice a one-year-old lamb, or, if they couldn't afford one like Mary and Joseph, two turtledoves or two young pigeons (Lev 12:6-8).

These laws make us squirm. But the purpose of Leviticus was to show very early in human history that the way to peace with God was by offering an animal sacrifice. In other words, we are unclean until something clean bleeds on our behalf.

These rhythms of Jewish life forced the people of God to grapple with their separation from God; to mourn their broken relationship with him; to ponder the same story told over and over by tradition–we need a spotless sacrifice.

So, Mary and Joseph take their baby, the lamb of God, to the temple for the first time. Before Jesus can walk or talk or even roll over, his faithful parents are obeying the law for him every step of the way. And this is just the beginning. Throughout his life, his death and his resurrection, he will perfectly keep the law given by his Father. He'll be perfectly obedient in our place. He'll live as Adam and Eve should have, loving the God who created them and loving the neighbour beside them.

We weren't born under that jarring law. We don't scramble after childbirth to have our children circumcised on the eighth day or strive to keep kosher laws. We hold fast to Christ's obedience instead of our own. We draw our life and our righteousness and our standing from him, instead of ourselves. When God looks at us, he looks and sees the beloved son in whom he is well pleased.

We can come to the Father freely and confidently, no longer relying on our strengths and our goodness, but looking to Christ's strengths and goodness that is
 infinite.

We can pursue righteousness in freedom, knowing that the fight against sin has already been won. And the day is coming when we will never sin again. Every day this victory breaks into the present a little bit more. Every time we are tempted to sin and we say no, we look a little more like Jesus. We catch a glimpse of what's coming. We will not struggle forever. The wait is almost over.

Part 2
vs.25-35

While baby Jesus is routinely received by the priests–who apparently do not know, or care to know, who this child is; two other inconspicuous elderly saints know exactly who he is. And they lovingly receive him, their long-awaited Messiah.

The devout and faithful Simeon has been waiting patiently, with great hope and expectancy, for the 'consolation' of Israel–for the Comforter, the Encourager, the Helper. God has promised Simeon that he will not die without seeing the Saviour, and the Spirit has assured him: *you're not going to miss out–the promise is at hand. You will see him–the promised anointed king, the Son of David.*

Every time he clocks a young couple at the temple, he must wonder, is this the one? It is by God's grace that Simeon has such faithfulness in his wait and such wisdom in his expectation. We don't know if he has waited a week, a couple of months, or decades. But just as the Spirit has been at work the whole way through this incredible story, he directs Simeon to the temple at the precise day and hour when Joseph and Mary are there.

Following the divine impulse, Simeon arrives and in one of the most tender moments in all of scripture, he lays eyes on the One he has been waiting for. With trembling arms, he holds the One of whom the entire Old Testament has spoken of. His heart soars in song as he praises God and declares that he is ready to die now. He is ready to be relieved of his watchful service and released from the heavy burdens of life.

The whole world stops turning as he looks in the face of salvation and feels the dimpled Prince of Peace squirming in his arms. Simeon's physical eyes see only a helpless baby, but his prophetic eyes see the salvation that is available to all tribes, races and nations of people.

Just as Mary and Joseph hold every word close to their hearts, there is a warning. Simeon rains on the parade of celebration that has pulsed through the narrative this far. He provides the first ominous hint that opposition will arise against Jesus and there will be judgment against Israel. When Jesus reveals the secret thoughts, people will be narrow-minded and intolerant. At the rebuke of sin, eyes will stare in stony silence. There will be particular hostility to the hospitality God offers to sinners, outcasts, Samaritans and Gentiles. And the salvation he brings will come at the cost of sorrow and death. A sword will pierce through Mary's soul as this son, this salvation, this rescuer, is put to death.

Simeon recognises that salvation isn't just something that Jesus will do but salvation is who Jesus is. He knows the consolation of Israel is not an event or a change, but a person. This baby who can't feed himself yet, who can't crawl or even hold his own head up yet; he is salvation. In his arms, Simeon holds the light to a world in darkness. He gently cradles the long-awaited Rising Sun.

Part 3
v.36-40

Like Simeon, Anna the prophetess is one of the few faithful remnants in Israel awaiting the advent of the Messiah. And let it be known, this woman is on a first-name basis with suffering and grief.

After the nation of Israel split at the end of Solomon's reign, the tribe of Asher went North and broke away from David's sons. And when the Assyrians came, most of the tribe were swept away without a trace in history. But a small group was left in the area around Jerusalem–which included Anna. Given her age, she was possibly in her mid-twenties when the Romans took over. And somewhere around that time, she also became a widow.

This dear woman lost both her husband and her nation– and the two may not have been unrelated.

Anna spent the early part of her life watching everything fall apart before her eyes. But notice her response: she dedicated her life to watching and worshipping. She spends her days in the temple fasting and praying and waiting, not for salvation through a band of anti-Roman thugs hanging out in the desert, but by God keeping his promises.

Despite her fragile age of 84 years (and potentially older), she never ceases to hope. Despite the tragedy she has faced, she finds refuge in the house of God. Despite her sorrow, she does not grow bitter. And despite her waiting, she never stops worshipping.

Anna represents the physically and spiritually hungry whom God promises to fill with good things. She is given wisdom about the prophecies concerning the Messiah and tells people of her expectations. And when she finally sees the promised Jesus, she abounds in gratitude having tasted

God's great grace in new measure.

Grace that will travel further than Israel; Grace that will burst out into the entire world as we see in the book of Acts; Grace that will come to all kinds of people no matter how unlikely, to people like us. This baby's sheer existence is the only evidence Anna needs to recognise God's redemptive hand in her waiting.

***

Here is the testimony of two servants with a full resume of life experience. Simeon and Anna represent all who see that their only hope is in the Mercy and Grace of God. Along with the humble carpenter, an obscure fourteen- year-old girl, and a bunch of outcast shepherds, they are flesh-and-blood examples of those to whom Christ comes. To those who are profoundly empty, yet profoundly full.

Both Simeon and Anna must have known the harsh life of living under the law. As they frequented the temple day in and day out, they knew the reality of their need for a sacrifice to end all sacrifices. But they were steadfast in their waiting, and they didn't waste their wait on frivolous debates or meaningless pursuits. They waited in worship.

Just as Simeon and Anna waited in hope for the coming of the Messiah, a similar hope beats in our hearts today.

In a month full of celebration and light, we often wonder why December is the darkest of all. Why does this time of year often feel so heavy? Why does it sometimes feel like the least wonderful time of the year? Why does it feel like we are wading through darkness? Why does grief sting a little more on the run-up to December 25th?? Why do we appreciate the December Disclaimers reminding us that it's okay if we don't feel *Christmassy*?

Maybe because celebrating the Light of the World makes the darkness of the world unbearable. Maybe we can't think about the Rescuer without thinking about the reason he came. Maybe we can't look Hope in the face without feeling every facet of the hurt around us and within us. Maybe God becoming a person reminds us of the person we've lost or the person we aren't.

Maybe feeling *christmassy* means feeling restless. Maybe it means feeling the pain of the world Jesus came for. Maybe it means feeling out of place and longing for *home*. Maybe it means feeling the grief of others and the depression of our own. Maybe while we think about Jesus' coming, we are just so darn ready for his next one.

Maybe. I don't know. But I do know on December 25th we can breathe a sigh of relief. Not because the Christmas hustling is over. But because the hustling, the anxiety, and the darkness do not have the final word.

Until then, we wait.

My own waiting often feels like impatience and irritation. My waiting is full of *why*? and *when*? I grit my teeth and try to sit tight until I can move past whatever my current trial looks like. I just want to get out of it. There have been many answers I thought would satisfy the *wait* in me over the years–a degree, a diagnosis, a father for my son, an end to physical and mental illness, another baby. But there is always something else. I am inclined to cling to answers instead of clinging to the One who gives them.

But by nature, God's people are *a waiting people*. Abraham, Sarah, the Israelites, Zechariah, Elizabeth, and Mary, all waited. And every single time God showed up with his steadfast and unwavering love.

Waiting really isn't about us and our unfulfilled desires but about God and his fulfilled promises. Our waiting shows us what truly satisfies–and it isn't the thing we're waiting for. It's him.

Friends, as the darkness around us deepens, and the moral and spiritual decay of our world suffocates our hope, it's more important than ever that we don't waste our wait. Turn to Jesus. Worship him. The One who kept his promise to come will keep his promise to come again. And in between, we can hold Christmas joy in one hand and Christmas sorrow in the other, because we are safely in the palm of the promise-keeper's hand.

The Son has risen. And someday we will rise with him. Until then, we wait.

Questions for Reflection & Prayer

1. I don't know about you, but I usually take my access to the Father for granted. I forget how Christ was perfectly obedient in my place from the very day he was born. In the mundane hustle of daily life, I forget that the fight against sin has already been won and it no longer has power over me. Take a moment to reflect on all that Jesus accomplished on our behalf. How does this motivate you to keep growing in holiness?

2. As we watch the waiting of Simeon and Anna finally come to an end, we can almost feel n our bones their sigh of relief. We usually want to grit our teeth, get to the other side of our waiting, and skip to the bit where we breathe a similar freeing exhale. But Simeon and Anna didn't get to skip loss and grief and sorrow and questioning. Instead, they worshipped through it. What does it look like for you to wait faithfully in the season you find yourself in? Is there anything you can change in your approach to suffering and struggle? What does it look like for you to wait faithfully in the season you find yourself in? Is there anything you can change in your approach to suffering and struggle?

3. Are there any ways in which you can practice the discipline of waiting? Consider fasting from something that will make you feel the tension of, *there's something missing here*. A small example of this is taking a break from screens on a certain day of the week. What rhythms of waiting could you introduce into your family life? We have no control over the *big waiting* when life blows up, but we can grow the spiritual muscle of waiting for when those moments come.

4. Throughout your Advent journey in Luke 1-2, what aspects of God's character has this study shown you more clearly? Does this provoke a change in your heart or how you live?

In our waiting, we can hold Christmas joy in one hand and Christmas sorrow in the other, because we are safely in the palm of the promise-keeper's hand.

An end of advent prayer

Lord, we are your waiting people. And as this Advent season comes to an end, we are more aware than ever before: it's you we are waiting on.

Thank you that in Jesus you stepped down into the darkness of this world, you left the splendour of heaven, emptied yourself and took on the form of a servant. We are so humbled to think that your arm rules over all history, all nations, all kings, and all circumstances and yet you took on human flesh, you experienced the darkness of the stable, the darkness of pain and temptation, the darkness of death.

Thank you that you conquered the darkness of sin once and for all. You were perfectly obedient in our place and your role as the saving, redeeming, creation-filling light of the world was secured.

You have called each of us out of darkness into your light. And everything looks different in the light of Christ. It transforms everything. It not only makes us see our sin clearly as foreign and ugly, but it also makes everything good in this world shine with its full and true beauty.

We long for the day that the light of Jesus will fill the earth as the waters cover the sea, but until then we are thankful that the light of Jesus helps us bear the pains of this life. His light is the lamp on our troubled path. It is the soft glow of peace that comforts us in our loneliness after a devastating loss. It is the light that reveals the wise and loving face of God behind every confusing providence.

As we move into a new year, may we remember that we can know your presence with us at all times. You feel every inch of this human life with us. For the weak, you became weak. For the grieving, you shed tears. For the low, you were brought low. For the broken, you allowed your body to be broken. For those who fail, you became part of a race of failures. For the shamed and the sinful, you became our sin and shame–and you nailed it all to the cross.

You are the desire of every nation; you are the joy of every longing heart. By your all sufficient merit, you have raised us and you will raise us yet. In our decaying bodies, we wait for you to come and right every wrong and reset every bone of your good creation. We turn our hearts toward you with all our loss and emptiness and pain and we say: come. We will wait for your good second Advent. And we will do so by remembering your first.

Amen.

Kid-size Devotions

Introduction

Can I tell you a secret? I think it is one of the hardest things IN THE ENTIRE WORLD to open only one door on my chocolate Advent calendar.

Every time I eat one chocolate, I can't believe I have to wait one whoooooole day before opening another.

Waiting is hard. I don't like waiting for my family to get home from work and school, or when my Amazon packages take two days instead of one.

Maybe, you find it hard to wait too. Maybe you wish you didn't have to wait a year for your birthday or an eternity for the weekend to come around each time.

But did you know God wants us to get really good at waiting?

Advent is the name followers of Jesus give to the weeks leading up to Christmas, and it's a time when we are supposed to practice waiting. *I know, I know*. It's hard to wait for Christmas. Can you believe people waited THOUSANDS OF YEARS for Jesus to be born on the first Christmas? Christmas?

The first time he came was pretty amazing, wasn't it? Well, the next time he comes will be even better. He will come to stay forever as our King and He'll make the world brand new, with no sin or sickness or sadness. Wow. Just thinking about that makes it hard to wait!!

The Bible tells us about lots of people who knew what it was like to wait a really long time, and throughout Advent, we're going to hear some of their stories.

WEEK ONE
Zechariah

Week 1 - Zechariah

Today, it's Zechariah and Elizabeth. When we first meet this man and woman who love God, they are super old and they don't have any children at all--even though children are what they want them more than *anything* else in the world.

By this time, God has actually been silent for four hundred years AND there are very mean men in charge of their country. It seems like God has forgotten Zechariah and Elizabeth. It seems like there is no hope.

But everything is about to change.

One day, when Zechariah is working in the temple, an angel called Gabriel appears. Now, this isn't the kind of angel you might see in your school nativity. This is more like a shining-warrior-messenger-from-heaven type of angel. In fact, angels in the Bible always tell people not to be afraid when they appear, which means they must be quite a shocking sight.

But not as shocking as the news Gabriel comes to deliver—Elizabeth, Zechariah's wife, is going to have a baby.

WHAT.

Zechariah finds this so hard to believe, he asks Gabriel for a sign. He needs proof. And boy, does he get his proof.

God makes Zechariah silent for a whole nine months. His voice stops working. He doesn't make one single peep until his son, John, is born.

God has a very important job for John—to prepare the way for Jesus. And the first thing Zechariah does when he finds his new voice is praise God for keeping his promise.

Zechariah sings a song, saying Jesus is the *sunrise* they have all been waiting for. Jesus is like a warm night-light beside your bed on a dark cold night. His light is like a cosy hug at the end of a long day.

Jesus kept his promise to come and he'll keep his promise to come again. And because Jesus always keeps his promises, we can wait with hope.

WEEK TWO
Mary & Elizabeth

Week 2 - Mary & Elizabeth

Last time in our Advent series, we talked about Zechariah and Elizabeth and their story of waiting.

Today, it's Mary's turn.

Mary, the mother of Jesus, also has a *waiting* story.

Way back in the Garden of Eden, when sin and sadness came into the world, God promised to send a Rescuer. And he promised this Rescuer would come from his chosen people. So, for thousands of years, every mother waited and watched to see if their baby boy would be the One.

But when the time finally comes, no one expects the Saviour of the World, the King of the Universe, the Rescuer, to come from Mary's belly.

Mary is an ordinary teenage girl, minding her own business and getting ready to marry Joseph. She is an unlikely candidate for the job. She isn't from a special town or a spectacular family. But Mary loves God, which *is* special and spectacular.

The angel Gabriel, yes *him* again, visits Mary and tells her she will have a baby called Jesus and Jesus will be the promised and long-awaited Saviour of the world. Unlike Zechariah who needed proof, Mary believes straight away.

If I was Mary I would think, *I can't do this. This is impossible.* But instead, Mary announces, "Nothing is impossible with God." Mary isn't strong and powerful, but she knows a God who is. She doesn't need to believe in herself, she just needs to believe in him. She knows he cares, and she is going to be okay.

One of the ways God cares for Mary is by giving her Elizabeth as a cousin. After she gets her super special news, she travels eighty-ish miles to the countryside of Judea to visit Elizabeth and Zechariah.

And before Elizabeth even has a chance to say hello, the baby in her belly gets there before her. Inside her belly, baby John does a big JUMP.

Unlike the backflips some mothers feel with their babies, Elizabeth's movement comes from a prophet who will prepare the way for Jesus. John the Baptist's job begins three months before he is even born.

The Holy Spirit helps Elizabeth understand why her baby is tumbling and she shouts for joy. She announces that Mary is blessed because of her faith in God.

Two women, two babies, two miracles.

Isn't it really *kind* of God to give Mary an older woman to talk to about bellies, babies and birth?

When Mary returns home, her heart and head are full of words from the Bible that she's heard at worship her whole life, so she turns those words into a song.

She thanks God for being mindful, mighty, and merciful—which means he is powerful and cares for her and never forgets about her.

Life will not always be easy for Mary as the mother of Jesus. Not everyone will like Jesus. Not everyone will like her. She will have to watch her son do hard things.

Mary is not what God's people expected. She is an unlikely person for the job. She is not big or strong or powerful, but she knows a God who is. She will not feel big or strong or powerful, but she will always carry the power of God inside of her.

As we follow Jesus and wait for him to come back, we also might not feel big or strong or powerful, but we know a God who is.

Week 3 - Jesus & the Shepherds

Shhhh, listen in! Are you ready? You don't want to miss this! It might not be Christmas yet, but in our series of Advent stories, we have officially reached the Very. First. Christmas.

This is the moment the whole world has been waiting for. Can you imagine all of the angels in heaven holding their breath to watch? Because, sure enough, the angel Gabriel is right once again, and nine months after he visits Mary, she gives birth to a baby boy.

It doesn't happen like anyone expected. The promised Rescuer isn't born in a hospital or hotel but in a shed. He doesn't sleep in a palace but in an animal's feeding trough. He isn't born to a royal family but to an ordinary teenage girl. Jesus doesn't come to defeat sin as a superhero or a soldier, he comes as a sweet, human baby.

Maybe, when Mary meets her baby she can smell the animals and straw around her. Maybe, Joseph her husband, lifts Jesus up and his first cry pierces the starry night. Maybe, she checks the breathing of the One who gave her breath. Maybe, the hands that hold the sun and moon in place, grab hold of Mary for comfort. Maybe, the voice that spoke the world into being, can be heard crying out for his mother's milk. Maybe, the Creator of the universe is born into a huddle of animals that he created.

But *why?* Why did God leave heaven and come to earth as a baby? Why did he come to be *with* us and come to be *like* us?

The answer? *Because we couldn't do it ourselves.* We couldn't close the gap created by sin between us and God. We couldn't return to the Garden of Eden or remove sin from our world.

So, in his kindness, God stepped down. He came as a child because God the Father wanted us as his children.

And because he came, he has felt everything we feel. He knows what it's like to live here on earth. He knows what it's like to laugh and eat fish finger sandwiches and hug a friend.

For those who feel weak, he felt weak. For those who feel sad, he shed tears. For those who are poor and hungry, he tasted hunger. For those who feel ashamed of their sin, he took our sin and shame to the cross and defeated it once and for all.

By now we know that everything in the Christmas story is backwards, right? Well, since Mary and Joseph are far from home and won't have many visits from family, God arranges a different kind of visit from some dusty-footed shepherds.

It's no surprise the first people who hear the good news are not in a palace, but in a field full of fuzzy smelly sheep. God dispatches is host of angels to a group of shepherds who are working the night shift—a group of shepherds whom many think to be a bunch of scruffy ragamuffins.

But that's not how God sees them. And before they have a chance to figure out what's happening, heaven fills the night sky with blazing light for an audience of shepherds sitting in darkness.

The angel announces the long-awaited sunrise has arrived (Luke 1:78) and then they burst into song. I wonder if it sounds like troops and troops of angels singing Happy Birthday. As soon as the celebration has finished, the shepherds drop everything and run. Hearts thumping and mouths panting, they move as fast as they can to find the stable.

And after they catch a glimpse of the promised child, the sunrise, lying in a manger–they will never be the same again.

The hard job of shepherding will stay the same, they will always be dusty, and people will always be mean to them, but God became human–and that changes everything.

When baby Jesus is older, he will spend his days quietly, going to work, getting sleepy, and living an ordinary life among ordinary people, weird people, and forgotten people.

Jesus became human so he understands what it's like to be human. Christmas matters in December, yes, but it also matters on an ordinary Tuesday morning in July. While we wait for Jesus to return, we can talk to him about anything, because he came to be like us and he came to be with us.

WEEK FOUR
Simeon & Anna

Week 4 - Simeon & Anna

We have finally arrived at the last *waiting* story in our Advent series, and it's a goodun'. Like all the best stories, this one starts with poop. *Sort of.*

Did you know that new babies follow a loose (emphasis on *loose*) rhythm or routine: eat, sleep, poop, cry, repeat. And did you know baby Jesus is no different?

Jesus' parents have this routine, but they also have another kind of routine to stick to—one that involves presenting their baby to the priests at the temple, which is kind of like church.

So, when it's baby Jesus' turn to be received by the priests-who apparently don't know, or care to know, who this special baby is; there are two other elderly worshippers who know exactly who he is—Simeon and Anna.

Simeon and Anna are two faithful servants of God who have been waiting patiently, hoping to see Jesus.

God has promised Simeon he won't miss out. He won't die without seeing the promised child whom generations of his family have been hoping to see.

So every time Simeon clocks a young couple at the temple, he must wonder, is this the one? We don't know if he has been been frequently waiting at the temple for a week, a couple of months, or his whole life. But just as the Spirit has been at work the whole way through this story, he nudges Simeon to go to the temple on the exact day and hour when Joseph and Mary are there.

And in a very sweet moment, he lays eyes on the One he has been waiting for.

This baby who can't feed himself yet, who can't crawl or even hold his own head up yet; he is Simeon's Saviour.

With trembling arms, Simeon looks into the face of his Rescuer and sees the light in a world of darkness. He gently cradles the long-awaited Rising Sun.

Like Simeon, Anna the prophetess is also bursting with joy.

Anna has had a hard life. She lost both her husband and her nation. She spent the early part of her life watching everything fall apart before her eyes and perhaps living the rest of her life feeling very lonely. But notice what she does: she dedicates her life to worshipping at the temple. Despite her sadness, she does not give up. During her waiting, she never stops worshipping.

Just as Simeon and Anna waited in hope for the first coming of Jesus, a similar hope beats in our hearts today.

Simeon and Anna are like all of us who know Jesus. Along with the super-old Zechariah and Elizabeth, the unlikely fourteen-year-old Mary, and a bunch of scruffy shepherds, they are real-life examples of the people whom Jesus loves with an everlasting, dazzling love.

In all of our own waiting stories, let's both walk with Jesus and worship Jesus.

If you enjoyed reading my words and you would like to continue the conversation, please get in touch! Picture me reading your response with a big dopey grin on my face. And then picture me running to tell my husband that someone read my words.

 www.rebeccasmyth.co.uk

 @rebsmyth

Front cover design and graphics by the wonderful and ever-so- patient Deyna Seffen @deyna.draws. Prints and colouring sheets by the equally wonderful and equally patient Lucy McClune @creationandthecreative. Formatting and techy things by the most patient of all, Paddy Smyth.

It takes a village to raise a book.

Printed in Dunstable, United Kingdom